*

MORAL

ADVENTURE

Perspectives & Possibilities

By

J. J. BHATT

ISBN:

9798835904693

Title:

Moral Adventure:
Perspectives & Possibilities

Author:

J.J. Bhatt

Published and Distributed by Amazon and
Kindle worldwide.

This book is manufactured in the Unites States of America.

Recent Books by J.J. Bhatt

HUMAN ENDEAVOR: *Essence & Mission,* (2011).

ROLLING SPIRITS: *Being Becoming /*A Trilogy, (2012)

ODYSSEY OF THE DAMNED: *A Revolving Destiny,* (2013).

PARISHRAM: *Journey of the Human Spirits*, (2014).

TRIUMPH OF THE BOLD: *A Poetic Reality*, (2015).

THEATER OF WISDOM, *(2016).*

MAGNIFICENT QUEST: *Life, Death & Eternity,* (2016).

ESSENCE OF INDIA: *A Comprehensive Perspective,* (2016).

ESSENCE OF CHINA: *Challenges & Possibilities*, (2016).

BEING & MORAL PERSUASION: *A Bolt of Inspiration*, (2017).

REFELCTIONS, RECOLLECTIONS & EXPRESSIONS, (2018).

ONE, TWO, THREE... ETERNITY: *A Poetic Odyssey, (*2018).

INDIA: *Journey of Enlightenment*, (2019a).

SPINNING MIND, SPINNING TIME: *C'est la vie*, (2019b).Book 1.

MEDITATION ON HOLY TRINITY, *(2019c), Book 2.*

ENLIGHTENMENT: *Fiat lux*, (2019d), Book 3.

BEING IN THE CONTEXTUAL ORBIT, (2019e).

QUINTESSENCE: *Thought & Action*, (2019f).

THE WILL TO ASCENT: *Power of Boldness & Genius,* (2019g).

RIDE ON A SPINNING WHEEL: *Existence Introspected, (*2020a).

A FLASH OF LIGHT: *Splendors, Perplexities & Riddles,* (2020b).

ON A ZIG ZAG TRAIL: *The Flow of Life*, (2020c).

UNBOUNDED: *An Inner Sense of Destiny* (2020d).

REVERBERATIONS: The *Cosmic Pulse,* (2020e).

LIGHT & DARK: *Dialogue and Meaning,* (2021a).

ROLLING REALITY: *Being in flux, (2021b).*

FORMAL SPLENDOR: *The Inner Rigor,* (2021c).

TEMPORAL TO ETERNAL: *Unknown Expedition,* (2021d).

TRAILBLAZERS: *Spears of Courage*, (2021e).

TRIALS & ERRORS: *A Path to Human Understanding*, (2021f).

MEASURE OF HUMAN EXPERIENCE: *Brief Notes,* (2021g).

LIFE: *An Ellipsis (2022a).*

VALIDATION: *The Inner Realm of Essence* (2022b).

LET'S ROLL: *Brave Heart,* (2022c).

BEING BECOMING, (2022d).

INVINCIBLE, (2022e).

THE CODE: *DESTINY* (2022f).

LIFE DIMYSTIFIED, (2022g).

SPIRALING SPHERES (2022h).

ESSENTIAL HUMANITY: *A Conceptual Clarity* (2022i).

MORAL ADVENTURE: *Perspectives & Possibilities* (2022j).

PREFACE

MORAL ADVENTURE: *Perspectives & Possibilities* explore the overall scope, "How to lift humanity out of its dependency from hedonistic life style, extreme techno aphrodisiacs and the systematic erosion of our collective identity."

MORAL ADVENTURE in other words is intended to the young minds that must learn of their respective potential at the core. Specifically, to make them be aware of their individual genuine moral strength to overcome many obstacles of existence; paving the path toward a meaningful future that is full of hope, harmony and durable peace, *toujours.*

J.J. Bhatt

CONTENTS

Fearless

Keep dancing
Even when thunders
And lightening keep
Threatening our
Big dreams

Don't be
Afraid it's just a
Momentary event and
Soon the Sun shall
Shine in return

Yes, to
Renew our
Possibilities and
Be the moral
Victors in the end

Let's just keep
Dancing with the
Will
That's so strong
At the core and
Let's be fearless all
The way to the end...

Being & Purpose

Past is
Always alive in
Our memories
And present is
Just spinning
Of creative thoughts,
Whims and dreams
As ever

It's
The future,
We often forget to
Think and
That's where our
Trouble begins

Though time
Is a man-made
Conception, we
Must deal with it
While in its hand

Before dissolving
Into eternity; we must
Fulfill our moral call to
Leave a world of good
Behind for the kids...

Truth
As Is

If the
Mighty
Universe is
Not static but
So dynamic

As it keeps
Exploding and
Expanding
Forever

The
Issue being,
"Why not us"

I mean
Why not keep
Expanding the
Self-consciousness
Toward some
Good

Even
Destruction and
Noble death is
Imminent in the end...

Reality
As is

Reality
May well be
Nothing but a
Hidden unity

Of all the
Infinite diversities,
Simplicities and
Complexities;

I mean
What the
Mind perceives
And dares to think
Beyond

Reality
Always an
Intrigued and
An intellectual
Mysticism to know
The real truth

Truth in turn,
But a big tease of
"Either/or" and never
A steady equilibrium
Of the human thought!

Identity

Mind,
Mission and
Nature all defining
The tangled state of
Existence

Mind
Always striving
To know all that is

Mission
Guiding the way
To understand the
Inner being

Nature
Nourishing and
Caring our dreams
To reach the highest
Peak, but

Are we still
Faithful to the
Meaning of our births
Or let death swallows
The essence for nothing!

Unfolding

Truth,
Is it either
A constant or in flux
From one generation
To another or what

Truth
Is it swinging
Between subjective
And objective ends and
Difficult to pin it down

Truth
Is it a mirage or
A genuine spark
Beyond
To be grasped

Is that
Why we're
Unable to seize
The experience of
Our truth or what!

Theseus

In the
Nineteen-sixties,
There was a movie
Showing a smart robot
Taking control over the
Spaceship; luckily just
A vicarious experience
Then

Today,
It is
Becoming a
Fast reality
Where smart
Thinking machines
Are silently taking
Control over the
"Spaceship Earth"

What if they
Call the shots and
Enslave humans to be
Nothing more than just
Paid consumer slaves
And let them be damned!

Confession

Solitude is my
Sanctuary to be
Free from the triviality
Of the quotidian affairs

It's the serenity
To the noble soul that
I hold with care always

Only in "Silence"
I am inspired to roll
Out my creative feelings,
Ideas, opinions and even
Crazy whims

That's my
Reality in the world of
Subjective interpretations
Of all that is

And along with it,
My times slipping away
So gracefully through
The life I've cherished
As always...

Half-n-Half

What if
We've been caught
For a long into a
Split reality

One is the
Concrete world of
Causality and other,
The inner being looking
Toward the realm of
Meaning yet to be known

We're
What a blend of
Double troubles:
Right and wrong,
Good and evil and
Perfect and imperfect
At the same time

While
Caught between
Life and death, we
Still are going through
Constant stirs of repeated
Blunders, sins and the
Cycle never stops...

My Lady

My Lady,
Yes my lovely lady
Full of charm to whom
I admire so much

She's
A pure heart and
Genuine being prefers
To live a simple life

Lady of
My luck always
So critical of I, but
She means it well and
I've just begin to know,
"Who she is at the
Core"

Lady of
My love assuring;
We're going to transcend
From here over there
Forever as One Soul...

Life
Force

Ethics
What a beautiful
Habit to hold on

From there
Flows the noble
Virtue of morality
And with it

Human got the
Chance to free himself
From despair, guilt or
Grief and reach the lofty
Realm, "What he ought
To be"

Indeed this
Juggernaut force,
"Moral Fortitude"
Yet to be
Lited in our time...

Earthly
Heroes

Why wait
For eternity to
Be merged into
Our joint truth

Why not
Be the voyagers
Right here in this
Magnifique vast ocean
Of struggles, pains and
Frequent killer storms

Let
The human
Mettle be tested
In its turbulences

I mean,
Through the collective
Determined will to win
The play on hand

For that is
Where we're the real
Conquerors of our gifted
Minds...

Aberration!

Being is a
Rational creature
Alright

He's also
Trying to be an
Awakened one

And, the journey
Seems longer than
What he thought;
Every time

Being is a
Moralist as well
And intends to act
Without a second
Thought,

Yet
Failing to do
So when the time is
Called upon

Oh yes,
Being is so smart and
Knows how to make it
Through without fulfilling
His responsibility to the
Good of the whole...

Worldly

Here
We're in this
New reality where
Everything seems
Changing so quick

In such a
Milieu of the
Modern time, there
Is no direction but the
Material consumptions
And life is greed-driven

And the
Rising shadows of
Ever expanding techno
Spells ; succumbing humans
To hedonism, solipsism
And jingoism

How far
The fragile
World can go on?
How far human
Can forget his
Identity while trapped
Beneath the thick layers
Of ignorance!

Excelsior

Let us
Rise in numbers
To be the fearless
Adventurers even
We're
Struggling through
The rough times

Let us
Indeed be the
Irresistible force of
Curiosity
To know the truth,
"Who were and what
We must be"

Let us
Be the
True explorers
And be bold to
Point upward
Always

And let us be
The winners of our
Joint destiny from this
Lofty heights of the
Ever ready spirits...

Voyager

In the beginning
Our finite mega-bubble
Aka the Universe was
Nothing but the tiny
One spark

And quickly,
The space grew faster
Than the speed of light
Along manifested, the
Four major forces

Leading to the
Creation of infinite
Stars galaxies and one
Definite among them;
The human in fact

In time he
Evolved from caves
To be the ultra ambitious
Space voyager; trying to
Know the riddles of the
Bubble and the self as well

And still he remains
An all-time voyager and
The journey never ends...

Epitome

From the
Lenses of
Abstraction,
Seems all is but a
Steady stream of
Consciousness;

Riding
The intelligent
Being from known
To the Unknown

He is
Very curious,
He is impatience
Albeit hesitant for
Some odd reason

Let him
Go beyond
Confinement, where
He is the manifest,
"Peace, harmony and
Hope of the whole..."

Enigma

Everything
That is,
Must be absorbed
By the inner mirror,
Only

The image
In it must be
Perplexing than an
Idea itself

Is it that
Image surpasses
The thought for some
Unknown error of the
Mind or what!

Oh yes,
Nothing
Seems an exception
From the imperfect
Three-pound thinking
Machine

That is why
Reality what is grasped
May not be the truth;
We've been after since,
The beginning...

A Flash

Karma,
The law of action
And consequence
Always a definite pillar
Of determinism

In Karma,
Every thought,
Word and a deed is
Judged accordingly,
Of course

And, they say,
"In determinism,
There is no room for
Morality as such"

I mean,
"Where is the
Rational convergence
Between determinism
And morality thus
Freewill into the mental
Equation, all we care
To know..."

Being &
Reality

Not important
What you do, or
Who you are, but
What have you done
Lately for the good of
Others is the measure
Of your character

Be sure
To use your time
Wisely and be the
Hero of your dream,
Vision and real experience
While you're on the way

Keep the
Spirit renewed
At all time
Keep the
Focus at all time

And be the
Total human before
Heading to the world
Beyond
Who knows?
"When will you be on
Another track again..."

Being &
Essence

Morality
Must be the
Expression of
Being's conscience

It must be
The very essence
To be human in
The full sense

And that is
Where his journey
Must begin to touch
The ever fascinating
Truth of the self

Yes,
That is when
Human is on the
Way to be larger than
Life itself

That is how
He is the spiritual-will
Linking him between
What is and what is not...

Know
Thyself

Since the
First step of human
Being on the road
Called, "Struggles and
Challenges,"

Existence is
Always an unintended
Consequences to say
The least

Idealism
For instance seems
Quite valid only
In the mind, but
Suddenly disappears from
The action-oriented
Reality

And the
Consequence is
Nothing more than
Another façade full of
Hypocrisy
Before the world alright...

Am I or
Am I Not?

Did I trip
Over the bridge,
Was it either intentional
Or accidental or what

Is it the
"Same am I" that's
Been recycled, *ad infinitum*
Or is it something else!

Why keep
Endlessly going through
The grind, if there is
No purpose to my existence?

And why
This experience
To be the link between
Life and death and then
Reappearance time after
Time

What is the
Meaning of all this
Charade and what is
The essence of my being

I mean, in this
Reality of uncertainty,
Anxiety and the tribal
Myopic claims...

Reflection

We alone
Must be the subject of
Inference of all that is
Yes,
In our beliefs,
In our thoughts, opinions
And overall awareness
To mention a few

Our
Premise always
Stands on a single
Assumption and logically
Arrives at some conclusion

But, the queries
Change with new discoveries
And we start the process again
Like the good old Sisyphus of
The yesterday

Nothing is steady
Nothing is permanent
And nothing seems to be
Answering to our collective
Adventure to experience the
Truth first-hand...

Unfinished Quest

The issue of
"Eternal Wisdom"
At times bit troubling
To think of

Especially,
When we're living in
A finite bubble called,
"Universe"

Again to this
Ever expanding
Mega-bubble,

We even
Don't know, what is
Beyond its observable
Reality, at this time

We tried
Superstations, myths
And Godly miracles
To know the assumption,
"The Eternal..." and
Still we remain
In the dark

Just take
A look at the world
Today and you'll know,
What I mean...

Two-Faced
Giant

Being
Sincerely holds the
Commitment of
Universalism of love
And care

As his inner
Wishes yet he can't
Get away from the
Myopia of his time

Being
What a believer in
Certainty of belief,
Yet he is a big gambler
In the game of life and
Death

Being,
Always his own
Voice of thoughts, ideas
And dreams, but
Stubbornly refuses to
Drop the old habits of
The seven sin...

Evanesce

Awakening
Without the real
Action is like an
Aimlessly spinning
Ideas going nowhere
In the celestial realm

Many great
Minds came and left
Tons of wisdom to
Rise above, but the
Billions failed to seize
It all

Well,
The struggles keep
On and seems, our
Humanity evanesces
From the scene simply...

Epiphany

In this
Constantly revolving
World of zillion ideas
And dreams by the minutes

Do us
Ever think,
"What is the blueprint?"
And do us care to grasp,
"What is the significance
Of the Moral Self"

Do us
Ever reckon, "Birth of
Human is not just a
Celebration, but the
Noble mission to bring
Good"

Do us
Ever realized the
Truth, "Freedom
Is not just an ideal whim,
But the solemn act of
Moral choice to be bold and
Genius to the end..."

Immiscible

This
Intricately woven
Reality
Where good and
Evil do coexists

Well
That is quite
Perplexing yet very
Puzzling, indeed
To take note

This
Divinely devotion
And actuality of
Human behavior seems
Quite disturbing as well

Again this
Coexistence of
Love and hate and
War and peace also
Paralyzing the total
Human freedom,
Life after life

No wonder,
Why the world is
Caught into a constant
Chaos, confusion and
The circular debate rolls on...

Inchoate

Make no
Mistake about it,
"We're the genuine
Sparks from the cosmic
Web of wisdom"

In time,
The magic sparks
Turned into an intelligent
Life and we emerged on the
Solemn scene at once

And the ancestors
Witnessed beauty and
Truth into the splendor
Of the celestial miracles

So they began
The journey to know
Everything all there is,
Albeit their eternal essence

Well,
The time has flown
By so soon and still we're
At the same point
As we still
Struggle to know,
"Who we're and what
We' ought to be..."

Synopsis

Our image
So shining into
The cosmic mirror
May be more than
Just a sensed-based
Notion

It's the image
Composite of million
Queries, riddles and
Paradoxes emerging
At the same time

What if,
That giant image is
A mystical projection
Of our greater meaning
Into the totality of all
That is!

What
Is It?

Birth
Gives a chance
To be worthy of
Something

Life
Is a real test of
Moral courage to be

Death,
Simply a passage
To eternity for
Whatever meaning

And we don't
Know, is it one
Or many cycles to
Go through or what

Only
Imaginations,
Intuitive thoughts
Or pure speculations
Keep us spinning from
Known to the unknown
And in between,
We remain stand still!

The
Flight

Let us
Soar like the
Imperial Candor;
Scanning
The whole terra
With its
Wide eyes and
Long wings

Let us
Like the awed
Inspiring bird,
Reach out the
Highest peak and
Know the truth
In time

A truth
That is
Illuminating
Being the very
Integrity of
The mind and
Nothing more to
Wish in return...

Soul Talking

The Soul asked,
"I am the enlightened
Fire, but where is yours?"

An intelligent
Being shot back,
"I am ready, but the
Seven-sin is in the way"

The Soul
Promptly replied,
"Well why don't you
Get off the old habits
And discipline the mind"

"I've been trying,
But the world is changing
Too fast, every time"

"That's not a good
Excuse to honor"

After a pause, the Soul
Continued, "Have you ever
Tried to reckon; what
Is the meaning of
Being human?"

"No, not really"

"Well, that is where
Lies your problem and
You better wake-up from
The prolonged slumber, now..."

Pure
Essence

Unity
Throbs into the
Very heart of this
Universal diversity

Unity
Is where all began,
Evolved and turned
Complexes eventually

Unity
What an eternal
Essence of all that is,
Indeed

Unity
Is the only way
Where separateness
Converge to manifest
As the final word

Oh yes,
Only the magic of
Unity
All the way to the
Ultimate quest called,
"Truth..."

Moral
Adventure

Life
Always
So capricious
As it dances
From a farce
Into a serious moral
Insight and lost
Human changes
In an instant

That is the
Power of
Epiphany
That is the
Strength of his
Will to win and

That is the
Best experience
Ever to be
Seized before it's too
Late to regret

Come and
Join the journey to
The world of silent bliss
And be
The master of your
Set destiny in return...

Meditation

Inner being
Wishes to go where
Creative experience
Is the existential norm

Yes, to the
Place where there's
No preaching, but the
Self conscience is the
Only wisdom

Let the
World illuminate
Where silence is
The real directedness

Time to
Rethink. Time to
Recollect. Time to
Know the future with
An open heart...

We're

All folks
Look alike with
A joyous attitude
Toward life itself

All folks
Feel the real
Humanity when
They're being
Treated well

All folks
Find their meaning
When exercising the
Moral will

All folks
Tears together
When bigotry, violence
And wars break out
At the same time

All folks
Carry the same basic
Dreams for their kids and
Loves to be in peace as ever...

Uno
Numero

It's the
Unwritten rule
Number one,
"Suffering is the
Prelude how life
To be lived with
Great caution"

It's a
Big challenge,
Of course
It's a mental
Readiness alright
It's a life written
With black and
Red ink and

Let it be also
The Uno Numero
To remember well
For a very long...

Voluptuous

Oh the
Lady of all the
Gracious beauty
And the ever so
Sensual pleasure

She's
Mercurial in every
Respect
She's a seducer and
A lady powered by
A pure self-confidence

Oh the lady,
Knows well,
"How hundreds of
Men are looking at her
With their fast throbbing
Hearts"

And in return,
She obliges them with
Her ever so tacit welcome,
A teasing smile and even
An inviting wink at times...

De Novo

How many
Times we've been
Reminded, "We're
The embodiment of
Spiritual freedom"

And, how many
Of us care to know,
"What is the significance
Of such an inner moral
Strength"

What is the
Pointing rotting in
This ever conflicting
Zone of ignorance,
Arrogance and false
Narration

Is it not
Time to wake up and
Get on the highway of
The moral fulfillment...

Know the
Way

Our grand
Story is primarily is
Constant conflicts and
Struggles for freedom
From oppression

Indeed, oppression
Disguised through rigid
Preaching's, stubborn "Isms"
Or a blatant tyranny; lately
Assault on Nature

As a consequence,
Rebellions, revolutions
And blood spills have been
The *leit motif* since we began
Writing the history

Only way to
Gain real freedom
Is to cultivate the mind
By having greater strength
Of moral grasp and rational
Insight and

Of course with
A deep sense of gratitude
To be born as intelligent humans
On this beautiful Planet Blue...

Reminiscence

Oh how I
Remember the
Bucolic beauty of
My village

Of course,
It was once a
Reality many moons
Ago yet so fresh in
Memory even today

Folks were then
Simple and caring
There was
Coexistence between
People, animals and
Green fields

And, never heard
Anyone got hurt
Either violently or
Otherwise and

Good life
Went on softly in the
Lapse of harmony
And peace simply...

Equipollence

Believe
Whatever you desire,
But never be the part
Of bringing the dark days,
Again

Worship
Whoever brand of
The Divine, but never
Kill anyone in His name,
Please

Accept
Whatever "Ism"
You welcome, but never
Destroy the dignity of your
Fellow human being at all

Salute
Whoever living hero you
May admire, but never
Humiliate another who
Has fallen for his/her land,
As well...

On
The Roll

Let
Life be enhanced
Through creativity,
Scintillating imaginations
And poetic reflections

Together
They offer a
Meditative experience;
Diving into the
Prodigious depth of
Many unknowns yet to
Be understood

It may be
A vicarious voyage, but
A worthy fascination
And new inspiration

Well that is
Where the mind
Begins to realize,
"What is it all about?"

I say, just keep your
Curiosity on the go
Yes keeps the gusto rolling
And be the active spirit
You've been forever...

Adscititious

When
Shall we bring
Together
The real and
The ideal

Yes,
As a first
Step to hope and
Friendship

For a
Long, we've been
Strangers; enhancing
Indifferent attitude
Only

Is it not
Time, we extend
Love and care
For a change

Let us
Be genuine
With our words
And actions

Let us
Be bold with our
Moral confidence
And be free forever...

Shakers
& Movers

Just
Erase the historic
Evil and rewrite new
Chapter of future full
Of beauty and truth

Let
Children of the
Present learn the Good
Of the whole and in turn
Be the greatest gift givers
To their kids

In such a
Grand moral cycle,
Death shall have no
Significance but the
Birth of every child
Would

That be
The journey we must
Be all on; redefining
Our common destiny
From this point on...

Defenders

Many times,
Life turn into an
Irresistible temptation
To let the will give-up

In such a
Situation, being
Simply descends;
Terrifying his very
Existence

Let him
Live for his true
Meaning
Let him
Be on the right
Track for always

Let there
Be clarity of his
Very essence
Let there
Be a set mission of
Unity and cheerfulness,
Only...

Nobles

We're born
To be the conquerors
Of our minds

Only then all
Other things and
Events shall justify
The journey we're on

That is the
Mission of every
Determined will

That is the
Glory waiting for
Every intelligent being

That is the
Path to the unknown
And that is the
Way to the Perfection
All we've been dreaming
For a very long...

Silent
Rules

Once in
Love, it got to be
Forever even it may
Or may not last

Once in
Harmony with
All others, it got to
Be the same either
Here or wherever

That is
The human nature
All right and the world
Carries it forward
At all time

Once
Awakened to the
Reality of purpose,
There is never a
Bigger surprise to the
Human experience

Once
In the deep state
Of meditation, there is
Never a disturbance at
The very core of the
Solemn Soul...

Moving
Force

Let's
Remember well,
"We're the owners
Of virtues and vices"
While walking between
Birth and death

Let's also
Remember well,
"We're the fulcrum
Between good and evil
While caught between
Our reality and dream"

And, such a
Reckoning, what makes
Us morally so bold and
To seek a meaning of our
Inner being

Just remember,
"Always to be the
Open-mind and learn
To know the trail well..."

Thrust

Through
This perceived
Reality
Mustn't we seek,
"Human and Truth
Are intricately woven
Fabric from the very
Beginning?"

To resolve
The issue, shouldn't
We atleast t try o be a
Rationally awakened
Spirit"

Our
Existence is
Solely dependent upon
How we endeavor as
One mighty force and

To know
The meaning of our
Collective will to be,
"What is our Moral Self,
Indeed..."

Cosmic
Gift

Oh yes
This wonderful
Gift of creative
Thinking

What a real
Jewel in the cosmic
Reality, indeed

It leads to
The deeper meaning
Of our purpose to be

It opens
The passage to
The world of million
Mysteries, riddles and
Infinite unknowns asking,

"What is the
Totality-of-Human-
Experience to be"

The
Path

Only
Reason and
Order ensures
A cohesive
Society

Where
Good folks
Across the board
Shall enjoy their
Harmony,
Peace and hope
For the future

Only
In such
An illumined
Milieu,
Folks understand,
"What is the truth
Of being humans..."

First
Magic

Where young
Hearts met and
Began to smile, laugh
With a joke or two and
The lights were off

As
Sweet music took
Charge and Maestro
Invited to dance

Well,
It was my
First dance at
The great event

My partner
Was a sweet gal who
Stole my heart at the
Very first burst of my
Deep feelings

We both were
Shaking with funny
Feelings; tried to kept
Them in check but the
Hearts were already
Silently so active within...

Declaration

Ours is a
A consequential
Existence

As it is driven
By the very essence
Of whom, we're the
Owners

In such a
Set reality of
What we know,

Let us
Be active with
Our collective
Reason and action
To spark,

A mighty
Experience of
Goodness
In the world

That's
Life

It is an
Excruciating defeat
To live with an attitude
Of unhappiness and
Keep dwelling into the
Tragedies of yesterday

Million
Stories, plays and
Poems being written
On such morbind event
But the life is just a
One big challenge for
Most to overcome

Let every
Being so born mustn't
Misjudge his/her ability to
Be smart, pragmatic and
Optimistic

For tragedies,
Tears, despairs and
Grief's be the shadows
That shall be with us
Mortals forever...

Winners

No need
To apologies
Any more

No need
To feel guilty
Every time

Just be
A Self-realized
Soul and keep the
Journey on

No need to
Know, "What's
Good and what's
Not"

No need to be
Posing someone
That you're not

Just be
A determined will
And stay focus with
The Noble Mission
You're born to be...

Every
Child

Every
Child born today
Be the illumination
To the world always

Let it
Be the moral
Necessity
Let it
Be the real
Mission to be

Every
Child who's
The future holder
Of big dreams and
Great reality

Let each
Discover their
Destiny to be worthy
Being born for a timely
Moral call, essentially...

Clarity,
A Necessity

Hell must be
Where ignorance
Is sovereign

Hell is also
Where suffering
Is ubiquitous

That's the
Reality beneath
All the surfacial
Cosmetics we've
Erected

Against such
Unpleasant truth,
Let us get busy building
Our inner better being

And shake-up
The hellish state
Where we've been for
A very long

Let reason
And moral will
Ride us out the killer
Storm from this moment
On...

Believe

Why burn
Into the fire of
Ignorance for
Nothing

Why be
At the
Mercy of others
Preaching

Why not
Be the
Awakened
Soul and

Know the
Trail well,
You're on

No
Necessity to
Know it all
When
The spirit is
Ready

To take
You all the way
To your own
Meaning...

The Mission

It is often
Said, "Death
Shall lift us all the
Way to the world of
Our real dream..."

It is also
Said, "There is
Infinite possibilities
In each human indeed"

In that case,
Don't you
Forget, "Who you
Are and what you
Ought to be"

Remember,
"That is the moral
Call to be steady on
The course"

Yes, that is the
Noble goal of your
Journey through
Thick and thin and

That is the pure
Responsibility of
Existence in short...

Force Majeur

We must
Affirm,
"We're
The force of
Change
In the world
For good"

We must be
Aware, "Life is
Brief; sneakingly
Slipping away by
The every sec"

Yes, we're
All on a roller
Coaster;
Riding
From birth to
Death

Oh yes,
Sometimes it's
Quite and smooth
And sometimes, it
May not...

Turning
Point

So love,
What happened
To your sweet promises
When we met for the
First time

Yes,
My love
What happened
To your vows when
We exchanged the
Rings

And, look at
What is happening
To our deep humanity
We thought we had it
Forever

All I hear
From my
Conscience,
"Why, why this
Betrayal when we needed
Each other the most to sail
Through the crisis on hand…"

Rethink

No point
In living for a
Long with no purpose
To go on

Not worth
Living life for
Hedonism and solipsist
Attitude at all

Just be a
Moment of your
Own moral spark and
Be the winner all the
Way to the end

Knowing
This world is but an
Ambiguity and uncertainty,
That's why it pays to be
A smart player in the
Game

Just get off
The wrong track and
Be the person having full
Confidence and rational
Goodwill...

Odyssey

A thought
Vibrating, expanding
Even exploding with
Alacrity to go on in
The quest of all that is

Let it
Radiate all the way
To the edge and rebound
With answers for which
I've been waiting

A Creative
Thought is the soul
Of everything we're
Looking into

For alone
It can appreciate
The order, the patterns
And the logic beneath
All that is...

What
We Know

Life
Not to be measured
By the personal glories
Or the high social ranking,
But the good done to
Others

Let
Life be a friend
And not a stranger at
Any time while on the
Trail

Life
What a miraculous
Experience to cherish

Life
What a wonderful
Image of noble death
To remember

Life
What a provocative
Memory to carry

Though sweet
And sour at all times,
Still so meaningful to
Walk through it all...

Evolving

We're
In this fascinating,
Fast evolving and an
Ever expanding world
Of innovations, new
Ideas and new dreams

Yes, indeed
We live in the holistic
Reality where connectivity
Is the magic glue and
Conceptuality is now the
Fact of life already

Wonder,
In such a highly
Interdependent and
Interconnected existence
Where is the room for the
"Freedom"

I mean,
Where is the place,
"A genuine human
To be!

Being &

Meaning

It's the
Only way to be
A spark of rational
Goodwill; inspiring
The young for their
Good

It's the
Only path to be
Walking along

Where
We're moral agents
Of positive change
As our truth

Don't make
More complex than
What it is

Just keep
The mission simple
Of the mind and go
On for an ever lasting
Light for the whole...

Mirage

History
For most part
Reveals nothing but
Million blunders and
Ridiculous sins

And in-between
For a brief; mankind
Made some spectacular
Progress as well

Yet, the pendulum
Remained more on the
Side of the negative forces,
Alright

Again, in our
Time, we've been
Witnessing both the
Awesome progress and
Mass suffering from the
Old wounds of yesterday

Wonder
What is the
Point of modern ideals
And sophisticated
Techno-advancements, if
We take one step forward
And fall two backward...

Action,
Only

Be bold,
Be your courage
And keep rolling with
Your head-up

This is
The moment to be
The force of history
And make the world
Aware, "Who you're
And what to become"

Stay on
The right rack and
Walk
With full confidence
And be the inspiring
Fountain to the young

Time to
Clean the augean's
Stable and lift the
Humanity to the peak
Of its dignity and
Glory yet to be...

Invitation

Come and
Take my hand
And roll along the
World of our happy
Dreams

Don't let
Fear stops you from
Falling in love

Don't let
What others tell
You, "What to do"

Let your
Inner being guide
You, "What is best
For you"

And decide,
If you care to accept
My invitation or not...

Be
Bold

Though
You're finite
Beings
You've the
Audacity to reach
Out the Infinite, if
You chose to-do so

It's all in
The magic of your
Determined Will

It's all in
The commitment of
Your moral confidence

Never doubt
The strength of your
Inner being, yes
Your very noble soul

And
Keep the journey
Going to catch the
Impossible dream in
Your time...

Upbeat

Even in this
Stygian night,
Don't think darkness
Is the king of all?

Look at the
Starry heavens and
See the billion
Friends showing
You the path

Yes, to the path
Where your glory
Is waiting to be saluted

Yes,
Where your wish to
Live in the right place
Is waiting
To be celebrated?

Don't fear
The dark and never
Run away from the
Stygian nights...

That
Thou art

Be the
Light
Through the
Dark and
Be a
Meaning to
Your life

That is the
Power of your
Success through
The thick and thin,
Always

Let
You're solemn
Soul wake-up
And
Let
You reach the
Truth

You've been
After for a very
Long...

Victims

Millions
Young would've
Lived longer

If they had
Not become
Victims to a few
Insane fellow men

Millions
Would've breath
Well, if nature was
Not disturbed by a
Few greed men

Millions
Would've been
Saved, if had the
Wise way to control
The deadly arms

Sadly,
Millions shall die
For the guardians are
Still ignoring the issues
On-hand...

Optimal

Self-realization
Is the eternal essence
Of every soul;

Wanting
To be at peace
Within and in total
Harmony with all
Others in the world

And that
Calls for discipline
The mind from the
Beginning

It's simply the
Good habits albeit
A mighty force to
Walk forward for a
Noble cause of the whole

When
The realization
Becomes "Universal with
No string attached"

Humanity
Shall experience its
Long waited dream,
Called, "Moral Truth
For sure"

Third
Eye

Spiritual
Path in essence is
The objectification
Of the Moral will

Let it stop
The world from
Chaos, conflicts and
Ignorance

It's the
Best human
Experience;
Lifting humanity
To the highest peak,
"What is to be
Being born human?"

It's this
Metaphysical
Journey needs fullest
Attention by the
Techno lost tribe of
The modern time..."

Artifice

Human nature
Is good and that
Be the premise from
Where we must take
The first step

It's
The positivity
Where
We win half the
Battle and keep on
Pondering the rest

After all
It's a human
Wanting to
Coexist in harmony
And peace
Only that way,
Civilization reality
Can live on for a long

That's why
Moral Education
Is a necessity for
We humans are the
Silent owners of the
Killer instinct at the core...

Give
A Damn

Today
Is the reality
To renew the
Sincerity of our
Collective will

Indeed, to
Clarify the way,
"How we want to
Live in a world of
Harmony and peace"

Yes, today
Is the day to rise
Above the insanity
Of violence's, wars
And the fear of
Climate change

Today is
To know,
"What may be the
Consequences, if we
Fail ?"
But then that is
Not an option...

Introspection

We
Humans the wise,
Why aren't we in
Harmony with others
Since the beginning
Of our coming

Why
Don't we know,
"Harmony yields
Peace and social stability
In the end"

And the
Glorious peace in turn
Grants us freedom as the
Best gift

Why
Have failed to grasp
Such a simple equation
Of existence

Is it
Either an eternal
Mystery or just our
Ignorance not knowing
"Who we're and what we
Should be"

Necessary
Being

While
Walking along the
Highway called,
"Birth to Death"

There is an
Incessant flow of
Thoughts, words
And deeds; making
Our conceptual
Reality indeed

Still we
Need the right colors:
Moral values, purpose and
Meaning and a rational
Insight to paint that reality
To its full beauty so well

Well it takes a
While to get the
Art work to be admired
By the billion viewers
Time after time

So let's be the
Best creative artists and
Leave something good
To many generations
To inspire with great
Admirations, we hope!

Journey

There is
Always a moment
To reflect

There is
Always a moment
To seize the
Meaning and

There is
Always urgency
Waiting for action

That is
The glory of
Being human

That is
The light of the
Soul to be on

Don't wait,
Just launch
The mission to be
Fulfilled in your time...

Transformation

Let's gather
All the loose ends
And tie 'em together
To see the whole picture
In the name of our
Collective sanity, please

This
Disintegrating world
Is the consequence
Of our mass ignorance
And we got to grips with
It soon

Why
Live in such Perceptuality
Of hatred, violence's and
Bloody wars

When we're the
Blessed Necessary Beings
To hold the torch of hope,
Harmony and the common
Sense...

The
Goal

We're the
Special gifts of
Nature
For we got
The power to
Be the sparks of
Eternal consciousness,
Forever

That's why
We're being inspired
To be the conquor of
Our collective truth
While being here

We've
The breadth and
The depth to go any
Point we wish to go
Either here or beyond

We got the
Potential and still
To be actualized it all
In our finite time before
We miss the train...

All in
Flux

Love
Is so sweet yet
So sour as well

Luck
Too is great wish
Yet not the
Whole answer

Life
What a great
Chance and still
Can be wasted
In no time

Being
Always a creative
One and still a
Destructive vulture
In certain respects

Time
What an inventive
Notion and still can
Fool us anytime as well...

Point,
Upward

The first level
Of awakening
Must be just the
Beginning

For
Being is still
Gullible to the
False narratives and
The pseudo-claims

At the second,
Being is half-and-half
As he still caught between
His own good and evil
Battles

At the third,
The highest level,
Where moral will
Awakens for the first
Time and

Voila, there is the
First magic experience,
"'Being Becoming" and
He's truly free, at last...

Builders

Why don't
We be the creative
Spirits; leading us
To the
Moral wholeness

Why
Don't we immerse
Into the perpetual
Solitude
To reinvigorate
Our habits of good

Let
The moral will
Glow
In the darkness,
That we're being
Caught into

Let
The world keep
Evolving toward a
Place of noble wish
We dream of it at
Every minute of
Our life...

Intrepid

Go chart
A new trail of
Great inspirations
And be the master of
Your destiny

Go leave
A footprint where
No one has been
Before

Be a
Genuine human;
Get to the mission
On time

Be the
Cosmic wanderer
And know the holistic
Truth of your own
Being into all that is...

Conquor the Mind

Between
The Godly who's
The One and many
On the other is
Not so important

And yet
Humanity
Being subjected
To many superficial
Claims, dogmas and
Sheer insanity since the
Beginning

Is it not
Time to walk away
From such hellish state
Of the mind and

Begin a
New journey toward,
"What is good to
The whole/"

The Crux

Pure and
Forever is this
Solemn soul,
What
A fantastic gift
To be worthy

Whilst
Life's just a
Brief swirl to
The being

That's
The big gap
Between what's
Perfect and what's
Not

Oh what
A spiritual
Spark is the
Eternal Soul
Whilst death
Just another
Consequence of
Human to be...

Moral Self

Source of
Truth is essentially
My moral will

From
There emanates
The power of
Awakening

Not thinking,
Imaging or the
Historic pages
Give me the bliss

It's the
Self-realization
That lifts my spirit
Above the spinning
Wheels of chaos and
Confusions

Yes, I do
Believe in mighty
Strength of moral
Insight and rational
Grasp, "Who am I and
What I ought to be..."

Long
Walk

That is
The Perfect
Thought

Where
Most humans
Desire to be
One with

Yes, that is
The conceptual
Wish to have a
Closure to the
Complex web of
Uncertainty
For sure

That is their
Pilgrimage
Yes, that is
Them walking until
Merging into
The Point Omega;
Either real or
Otherwise!

Where're
They?

Into
This techno
Twenty-one

Why are we
Keep falling
Into this
Hellish state of
The toxic
Whims, relentless
Laziness and the
Headless claims

Where are
The guardians
Pointing to the
Right way;

Freeing us
From the
Self guillotined
Experience...

Being
As Is

Human
Destiny coded
By growth and
Change simply

That is
Transformation
Of the monkey mind
From despair to the
Eternal hope in
Return

It's the
Renewal from
Birth to death and
Life again

It's the
Very essence of
Reality from one
Beginning to another,
Ad infinitum...

The Quest

Truth
What
An objective
Thought it in its
Pure sense

And that is
The expression
Called, "Unity"
For sure

That is
The first principle
To know well before
Launching
The ardous journey
We shall be on

That is the
Only way we the
Finite souls shall
Merge into the
Totality of all that is

That is the
Only way we shall
Grasp the meaning,
"Who we're and
What we ought to be."

As Is

Whatever
Little left over
Consciousness
After death

Must be the
Soul heading
Toward eternity
With no regrets,
I suppose!

Meanwhile,
New birth occurs
And in time the
Dead is forgotten

Well, that is
Reality of human
Memory and amnesia
Dancing at the same time

To that
We call the ephemeral
Human nature; always
Busy in his struggle to
Survive into the state of
Uncertainty of life as is...

Toward
Good

Be in the
Rhythm, melody
And meaning of
Your essence

Never
Swerve from it
For the trail's
Leading to the
Realm of myriad
Unknowns

Don't despair,
Don't be in grief
And don't ever quit
The scene

For you're
The power of
Positive change and

Must keep,
"Walk the walk"
Going no matter what
May be the consequence...

Stellar
Sparks

You young
At heart be sure
To seize the spontaneity
Of your inner being
At every turning point

Try to be
In the state of
Meditative thoughts,
Mostly to let you
Know where is the
Right direction to
Roll

Don't be
Afraid to touch
The world where
No one's gone before

Don't ever
Give up your
Moral courage and
Will to win always...

Being &
Freedom

Consider
The past is just
The eye opener,
But let the present
Be the mind opener

Yes, to
Shape the future
To be the reality
Born out of your
Big dream

Existence
Is a constant
Renewability of
The inner being;
Calling to be the
Enlightened soul

Always, be what
You are and keep
The journey going
Toward the set noble
Goal as ever...

Riders

Is it not
Time to leave
The narcissistic
Mirror and be
The rider of the
Goodwill

Is it not
Time to reckon,
"We've mission
On our hands"

Be careful,
Time is slipping
Away so sneakingly
And the trail is too
Long to cover yet..."

In Flight

At the deep
Structure of
Reality: God,
Life, Universe and
All other lose ends

Simply
Seems just a
Conceptual
Manifests to keep
Human sanity
In check

History,
Of course offers
Something else and
The fact remains

There is
Lot to be reformed
Before reaching out
To the distant truth

That sums
The great glory,
I mean the great
Story of humanity;

Still aimlessly
Spinning within
The matrix called,
"The suspended
Judgment."

A Perspective

Wonder,
If there is
An intelligent
Life beyond and

If in their
Thoughts if there
Something we call,
"God or what ever
Either rational or
Irrational would be
Obsessing their minds"

Suppose,
If they don't and
Still enjoy the reality
Of perfection what
We've been after for
A very, very long!

Would it
Mean we're on
A wrong track since
The beginning of
Our imagined
Collective superstitions,
Myths and of course the
Organized beliefs as well!

Inscrutable

If human
Enjoys the beauty
And harmony of
This cosmic, splendor
Indeed

Why does he
Fail to enjoy the
Same within and in
Fellow others too

That is
The big contradiction
To be born human

That is
Also the big paradox
To be deciphered yet

Try to be
The gallant spirit of
Moral action for this
Is the one chance
Experience in essence...

Dance

Oh the
Lady of my
Ever growing
Dream

Come and
Dance with me
Cheek to cheek
Under the canopy
Of this romantic
Night

No point
Avoiding the
Inner feelings
When the hearts
Have been already
Talking

Come and
Join me to the
Symphony,
"What is the
Meaning of our
Two waiting souls"

Oh the lady
Of my reality, "Why
Don't you join me to
Dance tonight
When zillion stars are
Smiling above..."

Sanguine

When
Cosmic inspiration
Is ubiquitous and the
Future throbbing with
So much hope

What's
The point being
Caged into the state
Of destructiveness
And the constant
Fear of death

Why
Hold onto the
Defeatist attitude
And deep anger

When
Life is ready
To roll a golden
Carpet
That is full
Of possibilities
To let you turn your
Dreams into reality
To be One...

Game Changer

When
Humans shriek
Their individual
Moral and social
Obligations

There is a
Terrible
Consequence:
Loss of dignity,
Even humanity and
Whatever is left
Over called, "Greed
And cruelty"

Social cohesion
Is a fragile state and
If not guarded; silently
There are recurrences of
Bigotry, violence and
The ugly wars

If that is
What we're witnessing,
Let's get smarter than
Who we've been and
Collectively attain the
Challenge as soon as we
Must...

Verdict

Life is
Good, but human
Needs to be reformed

The evidence
Is vividly shown by
The historic many
Millions deaths

Sadly in the
Name of good God,
Glory of man's ego and
Cruelty that all we know
So well

Yet,
Progressive humans
Refuses to accept the
Verdict and

The world
Keeps writing the old
Chapters over and again

Are we like the
Rats endlessly spinning
On the wheels of no return
Or what!

Return

The main
Thesis, "Let every
Born be engaged in
Becoming Good"

That is the
Only way to
Experience,
"Societal harmony
And ever inspiring
Unity to be"

Yes, human
Goodness is a
Necessity to make
The dream comes true

For it's a stairway
Leading us to ascend
From selfishness to
Selflessness and be
The generous givers
To the needy others

Let us return
To simplicity, spirituality
And be free from the
Overly materially oriented
Complex reality we've been
Caged with a long suffering...

To Be

It's the
State of meditative
Aspiration which
Transforms
Potentiality of perfection
Into the actuality

At that very
Turning point, being
Is enlightened Soul
Indeed

The Soul
That is ready to roll
Toward greater goals
Of the whole

Yes,
To bring forth,
"Harmony, hope and
Real action to be the
Best humans ever"

Remember,
It is the
"Silent Bliss" that
Yields the positive
Consequences to be
Born humans..."

Lost

All Truth
Must be solely the
Manifested conceptuality
Of the human mind and
Beyond it, we can take
A wild guess, only

Myths,
Religions and
Others got their
Respective notion
As well

Though there is
This common idea,
"The Eternal,
The Grand Unity or
The Nothing at all"

Are we
Essentially beating
Around the bush and
Nothing objective in its
Full sense has emerged
On the scene yet!

The
Drive

What if
Essence is laced
Over the thinking mind;
Pushing toward clarity
Of the unknown or what!

What if
Truth is sprinkled
Over the Silent Soul;
Driving it from imperfection
To the Perfection or not!

Basic issues
Emanating from the
Probing spirit and no
Day light yet

Keep the
Journey rolling forward
And be the fully-confident
Being, I mean
All the way to the
Fruitful end...

Self-Deception

This life,
This artifice of
All things and
This cosmic
Magic
Shall not endure
Forever

All of 'em
Are merely units
Of something
Much greater and
Whatever that may
Be we shall never
Know

While in
Existence we shall
Pray, "That Whatever"
Just to hide our guilt's and
The seven-sin only...

Renewal

Reality
What we conceive
May be
The very projection
Of human thoughts
Simply

And
Surprisingly,
Whatever is grasped
Through conceptuality
Turns into an objective
Truth

That is
How superstitions,
Myths and organized
Beliefs arrived to be
The human experience

Glad,
A few enlightened
Minds began to walk
Along a new path and
Sought for a deeper
Meaning beyond the
Emotive realm...

Simple
As Is

Let's face it
With all the sincerity,
"We humans are just
And good at the core"

We indeed
Are the masters of
Our destiny,

If we can boldly
Keep the cooperative
Spirit and carry the
Single purpose

To be
In harmony
With rest others and
Be mindful of children's'
Future...

Silhouette

Though
The dark shadows
Keep expanding under
The canopy of light,
Being alone is an
Incessant flow toward
His moral good

That is how
He shall justify his
Glowing essence,
All the way to the
'Self-knowing'

Let him
Relearn,
"How to get off the
Spider-web of rapid
Change and uncertainty
Of what the future may be"

Still there is
Little time left
To get off the mindless
Train; going nowhere,
But to the imminent hell...

Eternal
Q

Through
Induction I go
From specific to the
Universal

Whilst, through
Deduction I begin
With the universal
And draw it down
To the specific

Scientists
Prefer the former
And philosophers,
The latter

Either way
We build a frame of
Matrix allowing us
To know, to understand
To discover, if there is
Any truth or not

Millennia after
Millennia passed by
And the eternal quest
Still rolls on...

Judgment

Judgment
Must be weighing
Between 'What is
Right and what is not'

In fact,
It's the very act of
'Free Will' in reality
What we think it is

Life
What an open
Social stream; how
It's in a hurry to be
The mighty Blue Sea

Death
What an illuminating
Passage to the moral
Adventure

Where
Left over meanings
Disappear and may well
Reappear beyond
To be the deeper
Meanings leading to the
Real Truth...

Dichotomization!

Should we
Welcome subjectivity
To be essential for the
Growth and change or
Simply ignore the
Proposition at large

Our queries
Been innumerable and
Objectify, that is
Certainty seems
Not available at least
In our world

In such a
State of the mind,
"How do we launch
Our next giant leap
Forward with full-
Confidence"

I mean when
Caught between
The realms of the
Perception and the
Metaphysical wonders...

Base
Reference

What we
Think and what it
Really may be is one
Of the big challenges,
Alright

I mean,
Reality is a
Big paradox as
It is constant yet
In flux always

In such
An abstruse
State of all that is

How can
We be sure of
"The Eternal
Objectivity"
That we've
Been seeking
It for a long...

Pivot

A few
Decades ago,
We saw the famous
Movie, "Space Odyssey"
Where the smart Robo
Takes over the control
Well, then it was just
A vicarious experience

Today,
It's a growing
Possibility the super
Smart AI's will take
Control not of the
"Spaceship" but our
Lives

Not a good
Prospect to think,
But it's the reality that
We will be facing before
Too long

What if
We're reduced to be
Lazy paid
Consumer slaves and

Sadly forgetting,
Once we were genuine
Humans who fought for
Freedom, Justice and our
Basic rights...

What?

Mind, Mission
And Nature all
Building the web
Of queries, mysteries
And miracles of all
That we seek to understand
And to know our place in the
Totality of all there is

That is
The world where subjectivity
Is ever linked with objectivity
And where humans are constantly
Juggling to grasp the meaning
Of their truth

In such an
Unstable milieu where journey
Still half-way-half through and
The struggle to keep pace with
All the on-going changes is
Quite challenging to mention

Wonder,
Where is the direction
To understand the deep
Meaning of human into
The big picture of all that is!

Fragile
Reality

Once in
Love means,
To be in the
Memory
Lane forever

Once in
The cage of a
Blind belief
Means,
To be ignorant
Slave forever

Once
A trust is
Broken means
It's never the same,
Forever

Let's
Learn to change
The equation and
Be smart with your
Conduct forever ...

Steep
Climb

Truth
Either its here
Or beyond
That we're not
Sure

Opinions
Pop-up now and
Then and they
Don't make any
Enduring dent

What if,
Truth is a blend of
Empirical and
Metaphysical to be
One whole

How are
We going to win
It with our quasi-
Animal minds!

Dream to Reality

Let
My free will
Be the
Guiding light;

Riding me
To the distant
Realm

Where
I evolve
To be the
Force of Good

Where
I am
The new reality
Out of my dream

Let
My inner being
Roll the dice;
Carrying me to
The pure beauty
And truth as the
Finishing line...

Explorer

I stand
Before this world
With deep curiosity

As I intend to
Link-up
With the totality
Of all that is

I seek
To understand,
"Whats
The meaning of me
Who's running from life,
To death for a brief"

I stand
Before this wonderful
Experience as a human
Being

As I exercise
My freewill to know,
"Whats the purpose of
I, who's riding between,
Grief and joy for a brief..."

Confession

Am I
Dreaming or
Am I lost in the
Name of your
Ever enduring love

Times
Gone by and
The echoes of your
Sweet song still
Keeps rebounding
In my heart

Oh the
Curse of old
Memories and
The silent tears;
Ripping my soul
Apart

Go away,
Yes go away from
My world

Let me
Be free from
The lost love with no
Regrets now...

Toward
Future

In
The silence
Of my
Contemplation
All I reckon,

Life's
Still carrying
Million scattered
Debris of riddles,
Dreams and wishes,
But no true action to
Resolve the issues of
The time

In
The silence
Of my left over time,
I look at the
Young minds and still
Retain hope,

They
Shall carry the
Torch to define their
Common destiny with
Moral intention simply...

Winding Trail

Absurdity
Seems a constant
Music in the
Background

Only the
Sparks of meaning
Fly now and then
In his inner being

That too
For a while and
Human struggles
Still so stubbornly
Along the trail

That is
The very
Experience to be
Human indeed

What
A challenge
While walking along
The slippery road of
The Big Dream...

Beware

Be mindful
If you're certain
"Self-identity" in
The world of rapid
Change

Don't
Let the reality
In flux steal your
Integrity of the mind

I mean,
The world where
Moral values
And rational insights
Are heading in wrong
Direction and

Meanwhile
We, the humanity
Simply passively
Stands at the very
Expense of our glory,
Our story and the
Future to be...

First
Step

Let
Morality
Be the
Shield and let
Reason
Be the sword

To resolve
Chaos and falsity
That has been real
Evil at the core

Only
Good conduct
Shall be the
First step

Yes
To live in a
World of
Inspiration and
The right vision
That we all seek...

Indomitable

Human
What a
Quintessential
Expression of true
Humanity always

Albeit he is a
"Self-conscious
Warrior" who's
Active in the moral
Confrontation with
His own inner being
As he evolves with time

And as he
Encounters series
Of choices: love, life,
Belief,
Death or beyond;
Facing the
Ethical challenge
Every time

If he
Succeeds in each
Battle; emerging
A genuine hero, but
Remember well,
It's an ardous
Journey, alright...

Authentic

To be
Self-reliant and
Will to act while
On the track

Yes,
To leap forward
With courage and
Compassion;
Carrying the
Unknown
Mission on hand

Let it
Be every human's
'Self- determination'
Let it
Be every soul's
'Eternal Inspiration'

No matter
What but in the end
He must
Define the destiny with
Clarity of the noble
Good always...

Love

Forever

Love is
All we got and
That's the life
We must

Love is
What the souls
Been and
That's the big
Win alright

Love
What a magic
That blended our
Dreams in reality

So darling,
We've been on the
Royal road for a
Long and now the
Time is ending,
But ready

To let us
Go beyond and
Be the lovers in
Eternity only...

Off the
Track

Why have
We fallen into
The trap,
"To be
Happy is to
Be smart winners
In the game of the
Seven sin"

Why haven't
We learn yet
From the past,
"False narratives
And pseudo-worships
Do inflict violence's,
Wars and many million
Deaths too..." and

Why have
We forgotten
The simple truth,
"To be moral is
To be the best
Human strength for
Harmony and hope..."

The Rule

All is
Transitory,
Even the journey
Between what is
And what is not

All is
Fleeting events
Keeps spinning in
The judgment wheel
Either, or

That is
The rule of the game
Driven by the twin
Forces: Good and Evil

That is
Existence itself;
Demanding to walk
Through it with
Caution, but with
Calm and
Full-confidence

Know the
Terra

Life
What a big bubble
Full of lies, deceptions
And sprinkled with
Some sincerity and
Integrity in-between

Love
What a big jar
Full of sweet and
Sour goodies, egos
And insecurity spiced
With some joy and
Grief in-between

Techno
Global reality
Either a great hope
Of humanity or a
Worse nightmare of
Tomorrow

It's good
To measure the
Past, the present and
To know what would
Be the consequences
In future...

Swimmers

Sadly,
When a being is
Alienated from the
Inner spirit and

Keeps
Sinking into
The world of
Flesh, envy and
Greed

He is
No longer
In reality, but lost
Into another place
Where confusion,
Despair and death
Waits

That's why
Keep the perspective
Intact and seek to know
Possibilities, "How to
Beat the odds against
Your survival first and
Success the second good..."

L'amoura

When
In love
Everything is
But lovely lyrics,
Music and dance

It's
A beautiful
Experience
It's
A fountain
Refueling feelings
Over and again

Love
Where dreams
Are emanated with
Great expectation

Love
What a necessity
To turn the
Dream into reality
Indeed

Love,
What a bold
Adventure to be...

Great
Walk

Let the
World reverberate
With the simple
Declaration:

"To be moral is
To be the
Universal measure
Of truth itself within"

Only then
We shall discover
Our original moral
Being
Yes the genuine
Image of every soul

Come
Just don't stand
In those thick clouds
Of ignorance

Instead,
Lets soar higher than
Ever before and be the
Freewill's
We're meant to be...

Ultimate

Intrigued
Yes, of course
And yet the call
Of enlightenment
Keeps spinning within
For some reason

The soul
Demanding every
Now and then,

"Be
The warrior of
Noble Truth and
Define the destiny
Accordingly"

That's the
Inner message,
To any willing human,
"To be moral means
To be a universal measure
Of Good itself, *in toto*..."

Great
Mission

Multitudinous
We may be
Yet we seek
Unity with every
Thing that exists

That's the
Common thread
Of our humanity
At the core

Let us
Be the glow
Let us
Be hope and
Harmony

Whatever
Is the enigma
Just walk together
And be the synergy
All the way to the
Mission called,
"To conquor the
Mind..."

Illuminators

We're
The ebb and
Flow
Recurring since
The beginning

Either
It's just highs
And lows or
Grief and joy called,
Unstable existence

We're
The presence
Simply
And don't know
Whats the future
To be

Whatever
Time is left over
In-between is our
Precious life

A life
Where we're born
To fulfill all dreams,
But they're meaningful;
If emerging as our
Moral reality, only...

Mystical Being

What is
To be grasped
While chugging
Along the highway
Of many unknowns
Still keeps revolving
In the mind

I mean, what is
To be identified
Is not just concrete
Particular, but the
Abstracted universal

I know
That's the giant
Leap from the myopic
Mindset to the totality
Of all that is

I know
That's the
Greatest challenge
But this life is my
Chance only...

JAGDISH J. BHATT, PhD
Brings 45 years of academic experience
including a post- doctorate research scientist
at Stanford University, CA. He holds an
impressive authorship of 50 books.

Made in the USA
Columbia, SC
02 September 2022